WHOOSH!

WILE E. COYOTE
EXPERIMENTS WITH
FLIGHT
AND
GRAVITY

by MARK WEAKLAND
illustrated by ALAN BROWN

CAPSTONE PRESS
a capstone imprint

Published in 2017 by Capstone Press
A Capstone Imprint
1710 Roe Crest Drive
North Mankato, Minnesota 56003
www.mycapstone.com

Library of Congress Cataloging-in-Publication Data
Library of Congress Cataloging-in-Publication data is available on the Library of
Congress website.
ISBN 9781515737322 (library binding)
ISBN 9781515737360 (paperback)
ISBN 9781515737483 (eBook (pdf))

Editorial Credits
Michelle Hasselius, editor; Ashlee Suker, designer; Steve Walker, production specialist

Capstone Press thanks Paul Ohmann, PhD, Associate Professor of Physics at
the University of St. Thomas for his help creating this book.

TABLE OF CONTENTS

It's a Bird!

It's a bird, it's a plane, it's … a flying coyote! But not for long. Wile E. wants more than anything to catch Road Runner. But to do it, he needs to make better use of science.

Coyote
(Hungrius carnivorii)

Road Runner
(Speedius birdius)

Anything that flies must fight against **gravity**. Gravity is a force that is always working to bring things down. Birds beat gravity every day. So do mosquitoes. But people and coyotes can't fly. To overcome gravity, they have to use science.

Wile E. is learning this the hard way. To stay up longer and come down softer, he needs lessons on gravity and flight. Let's get him started.

gravity—a force that pulls objects with mass together; gravity pulls objects down toward the center of Earth

CHAPTER 1

GO WILE E., GO!

Speed

A roller-blading coyote? You may see stranger things before this is all over. To get ready to fly, Wile E. must learn about **speed**. Speed is how fast an object moves at any given moment. As Wile E. moves across the desert, he travels at a constant speed. Right now his speed is 3 meters per second, or 3 m/s.

Wile E. can see that Road Runner is faster than he is. To increase his speed, Wile E. adds more force. The force comes from moving his legs. Unfortunately for Wile E., Road Runner can apply force too. Even a hard-working, roller-blading coyote can't catch that bird.

speed—rate of motion or progress

Velocity

To avoid a shocking situation, a flying coyote needs to know about **velocity** as well as speed. Velocity is the rate of change in an object's position. Think of it as speed with a direction. Let's say Wile E. is moving at 50 m/s, and he is flying east. Wile E.'s velocity is 50 m/s, east. When Road Runner changes direction and runs south, Wile E. changes direction too. Now Wile E.'s velocity is 50 m/s, south.

velocity—the speed an object travels in a certain direction

During a flight, the pilot always knows the plane's velocity. He or she also knows the velocity of the wind blowing on the plane. Knowing both helps the pilot plan for a smooth and safe flight.

Wile E. can change his velocity while flying. In other words, he can change his speed and direction. When Road Runner speeds up and heads west, Wile E. increases his speed and changes direction. But he forgot to fly higher off the ground. ZAP!

Velocity and Acceleration

Back on the ground, Wile E. is getting a lesson on **acceleration**. Wile E. uses the force of his legs to push himself across the flat desert. When he comes to a hill, he stops pushing. If Wile E. is no longer pushing, why does he keep moving? He moves because the force of gravity is pulling him. As gravity pulls, Wile E. gains speed. Soon he is rolling faster and faster down the hill. Wile E.'s direction is also changing. Now he is moving south instead of west.

acceleration—a change in velocity

A change in speed or direction is a change in velocity. A change in velocity is called acceleration. Acceleration can happen to anything that moves, such as a car, plane, or rolling coyote. Look out below!

OH NO!

CHAPTER 2

GRAVITY BRINGS YOU DOWN

Gravity Is a Force

Poor Wile E. doesn't know how strong Earth's gravity is.
Every object in the universe has gravity. Tiny grains of sand have
gravity. So do planets and stars. All objects on Earth experience
gravity as a constant acceleration toward the center of the planet.
It doesn't matter how heavy or light they are.

On Earth, objects fall at a constant acceleration of 32 feet (9.8 meters) per second squared. All objects, from feathers to bricks to coyotes, increase their speed as they fall by 32 feet (9.8 m) per second, every second.

If astronauts in a spaceship were accelerating through deep space, they would experience a force just like Earth's gravity. Scientist Albert Einstein discovered this more than 100 years ago.

Did you know that there is only a small amount of gravity in outer space? Gravity keeps the moon orbiting Earth and Earth orbiting the sun. When people and objects orbiting Earth seem to be weightless, it's called microgravity. They are in "free fall" as they go around Earth, which causes the feeling of weightlessness.

Gravity on Other Planets

Wile E. decides to try out gravity on the moon!
Other planets and moons have gravity too. But the
amount of gravity depends on mass. A planet or moon
with a small mass has a small amount of gravity.

For example, Earth's moon has about 81 times less mass than Earth. It is also smaller in size. This means the smaller and lighter moon has a lot less gravity. When Wile E. and Road Runner stand on the moon, they experience a small amount of the pulling power that gravity has on Earth.

Wile E. isn't thinking about the moon's weaker gravity. When he pushes the boulder, it slowly falls to the ground. Road Runner has plenty of time to get out of the way!

CHAPTER 3

UP, UP, AND AWAY

Counteracting Gravity

Wile E. thinks Earth's gravity is easier to deal with. Back on Earth when Wile E. leaps, gravity takes over and pulls him down. Wile E. needs a strong force to work against gravity. He has chosen air **resistance**.

Air resistance, or drag, is a force that slows an object's fall. To see drag in action, drop a paper clip and a sheet of paper. Because gravity gives constant acceleration no matter the object's mass, both the paper clip and paper should hit the ground at the same time. The paper clip doesn't have a lot of drag, so it falls at a typical rate. But the sheet of paper has more surface area. This creates a lot of drag. Drag slows the paper's fall.

Just like the sheet of paper, Wile E.'s parachute creates drag.
This slows his fall. When a strong gust of wind blows into his
parachute, another force acts on it. This force is called **lift**. Lift
works against gravity. Wile E. rises, and his plan is ruined.

lift—the upward force that causes an object to rise in the air

resistance—a force that opposes or slows the motion of an
object; friction is a form of resistance

Air Speed and Lift

Wile E. knows that birds and airplanes beat gravity every day. And he thinks a coyote can too. A pair of wings should give Wile E. the lift he needs to beat gravity and get off the ground.

Wings work by moving the air around them. Wile E.'s plane wings push more and more air away as they pick up speed. Even more air moves when Wile E. moves the wings in a specific direction.

Lift presses up on an airplane's wings as air is increasingly moved away. All this upward pressure forces the wings and Wile E. into the sky. Wile E. is flying!

Of course if the wings are damaged, they won't work correctly. No wings mean no lift. And no lift means that gravity pulls the plane and Wile E. to the ground.

pressure—exertion of force upon a surface; force per unit area

CHAPTER 4

FLYING FORCES

Lift and Weight

Gravity constantly acts on Wile E.'s plane. But other forces act on it as well. Lift is one force. When Wile E. sits on the ground, he has no lift. But he does have weight, which is caused by his mass in the presence of gravity. To move his weight and the weight of his plane off the ground, Wile E. drives his plane forward. As the wings push away the air, they create lift.

lift

gravity

As Wile E.'s plane goes faster and faster, more and more air is pushed away. Air pressure increases under the wings. Soon lift will exceed gravity. When this happens, the plane rises. As long as Wile E. keeps a high enough air speed, the plane will stay in the air.

So why does Wile E. crash? As he slows down to net Road Runner, his plane loses lift. Soon there is not enough lift to overcome gravity.

Drag and Thrust

You can't keep a good coyote down. This time Wile E. won't slow his plane's speed. He'll also use a bigger engine, which will make more **thrust**.

Thrust and drag are two more forces that act on Wile E.'s plane. A plane's engine creates thrust. Thrust moves the plane forward down the runway and through the air. Drag works against thrust. It comes from the air resistance that pulls on the plane as it moves through the air. If the plane's engine thrust is greater than the air's drag, the plane accelerates forward. But if the drag becomes too great, the plane slows down.

drag

thrust

thrust—the force that pushes a vehicle forward

Pilots pull in a plane's wheels when flying. They do this for the same reason birds tuck in their legs. Legs and wheels create drag, which slows them down. When Wile E. gets ready to use his capture box, the box creates a lot of drag. This slows the plane down and allows Road Runner to get away. What a drag!

Equilibrium

Wile E. has learned that lift, gravity, thrust, and drag are the forces acting on his plane. All four forces must be balanced for a steady flight. When all the forces are balanced, they are in **equilibrium.**

When they are not in equilibrium, any number of things can happen. If the thrust is greater than the drag, the plane accelerates forward. If the drag is greater than the thrust, the plane slows down. If lift is greater than gravity, the plane accelerates upward. And if gravity is greater than lift, the plane accelerates downward.

equilibrium—a state of balance due to the equal action of opposing forces

Now Wile E. can relax. Even with the capture box, he is having a steady flight. Of course, there is more to flying than just forces. Wile E. needs to watch where he's going!

Orbital Velocity

It's Wile E. Coyote, rocket scientist! He's learned that some flying machines don't have to deal with four forces.

Only three forces act on a rocket during takeoff. A rocket flies straight up and does not need wings to provide lift. So a rocket only deals with thrust, gravity, and drag. Gravity and drag hold the rocket down. Thrust moves it upward.

To get into orbit, a spacecraft must move upward very quickly. This is called **orbital velocity**. On Earth, the orbital velocity is around 7,800 m/s. That's 17,600 miles per hour!

ON HO!

ACME CORPORATION

BEEP BEEP!

Once in space, only gravity and thrust act on a spaceship. Lift and drag do not factor into a ship's flight because there is no air in space. Hopefully Wile E. will jump off before he gets that high!

orbital velocity—the speed an object needs to reach in order to orbit Earth

Wile E. looks a bit down, don't you think? Even though things aren't looking up for him, Wile E. has learned a lot. He knows acceleration is a change in velocity. He knows gravity is a force. He understands that all objects experience gravity. He sees that gravity and drag bring things down. And he knows that lift and thrust help birds and planes fly. It looks like Wile E. could use a little lift right now!

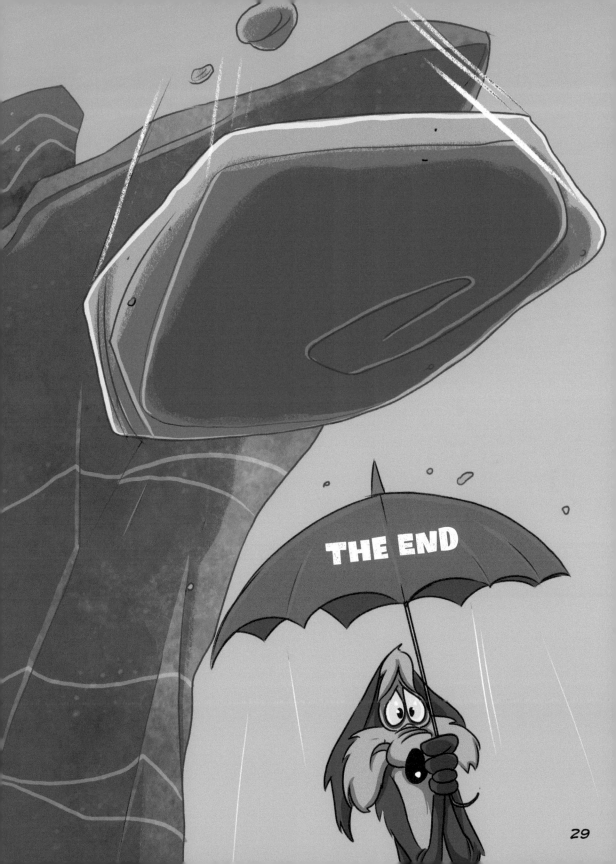

GLOSSARY

acceleration (ak-sel-uh-RAY-shuhn)—a change in velocity

equilibrium (ee-kwuh-LIB-ree-uhm)—a state of balance due to the equal action of opposing forces

gravity (GRAV-uh-tee)—force that pulls objects with mass together; gravity pulls objects down toward the center of Earth

lift (LIFT)—the upward force that causes an object to rise in the air

mass (MASS)—amount of matter in an object

orbital velocity (OR-bit-uhl vuh-LOSS-uh-tee)—the speed an object needs to reach in order to orbit Earth

pressure (PRESH-ur)—exertion of force upon a surface; force per unit area

resistance (ri-ZISS-tuhnss)—a force that opposes or slows the motion of an object; friction is a form of resistance

speed (SPEED)—rate of motion or progress

thrust (THRUHST)—the force that pushes a vehicle forward

velocity (vuh-LOSS-uh-tee)—the speed an object travels in a certain direction

READ MORE

Nahum, Andrew. *Flight.* DK Eyewitness Books. New York: DK Pub., 2011.

Royston, Angela. *Forces and Motion.* Essential Physical Science. Chicago: Capstone Heinemann Library, 2014.

Spilsbury, Louise. *Flight.* The Science Behind. Chicago: Raintree, 2012.

INTERNET SITES

FactHound offers a safe, fun way to find Internet sites related to this book. All of the sites on FactHound have been researched by our staff.

Here's all you do:

Visit *www.facthound.com*

Type in this code: 9781515737346

Check out projects, games and lots more at
www.capstonekids.com

INDEX

OTHER BOOKS IN THIS SERIES

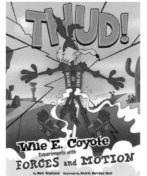

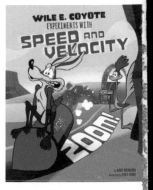